Pin and thread craft

Pin and thread craft

Warren Farnworth

B T BATSFORD LIMITED
London

© Warren Farnworth 1975
First published 1975
Reprinted 1975
ISBN 0 7134 2898 8

Filmset by Servis Filmsetting Ltd, Manchester
Printed in Great Britain at The Pitman Press, Bath
for the publishers B T Batsford Limited
4 Fitzhardinge Street London W1H OAH

Contents

Acknowledgment   6

Introduction   7

Principles of linear design   9
Regular shapes   18
Circles   28
Spirals   34
Polygons   36
Moiré patterns   40
Curve stitching   42
Representational design   52

Linear design with threads and wire   60
Working drawings   62
Panel materials and preparation   62
Surface treatments   63
Pins and nails   67
Wire and thread   68

Development of linear design   74
Other linear materials and material
treatments   74
Other graphic media   75
Other support materials   75
Other methods of fastening   78
Linear design in three dimensions   82

Nail art   87

Suppliers   95
Kit suppliers   96

Acknowledgment

The author and publishers would like to thank the
following for their kind permission to reproduce
illustrations in this book:
Peter Collingwood for figure 96
The Camera Press Limited for figures 115 and 116
Jennifer Gray for figures 78, 79 and 84
Pan Am, New York, for figure 107
John M Pickering for figure 120
Edward Rogers and Thomas Sutcliffe for figure 101
The Trustees of the Tate Gallery, London, for
figures 87, 104, 118 and 119

Introduction

1

Here is an introduction to the practice of linear design and, in particular, to the creative use of threads and wire, held in place with pins or nails – the kind of work illustrated in figure 1. As such, it is an introduction to a technique and an art form which is pertinent equally to the young school child and the professional craftsman.

It is at once both simple and complex. Simple, inasmuch as a young child might easily adapt the technique, using elastic bands on a pegged board: complex to the extent that a finely-executed panel requires considerable judgment and skill. Yet it is precisely this duality which makes the practice such a valuable one. It can be pursued at all levels. Moreover, it is a practice which can extend to relate variously to graphic design, scupture, painting, collage, weaving and printmaking; areas which cannot be treated fully here, but which any educational programme must bear in mind.

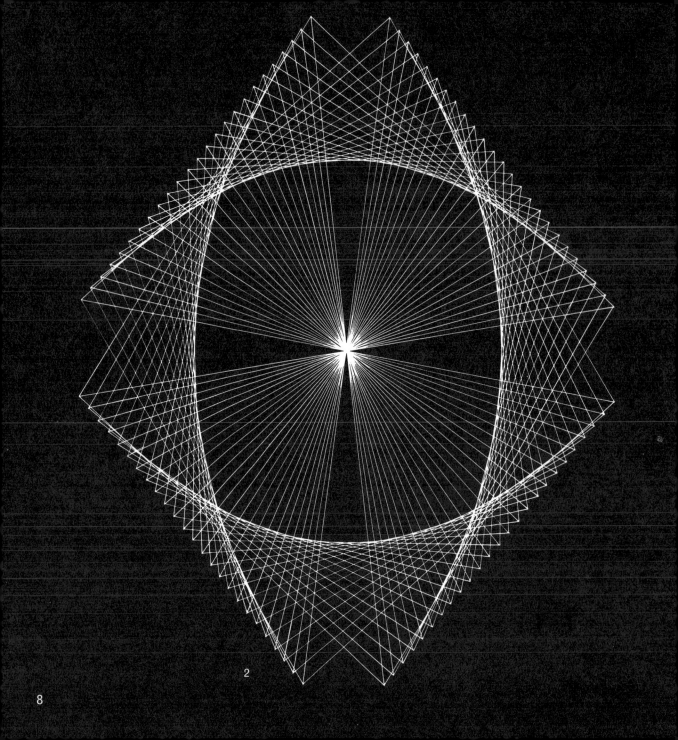

2

Principles of linear design

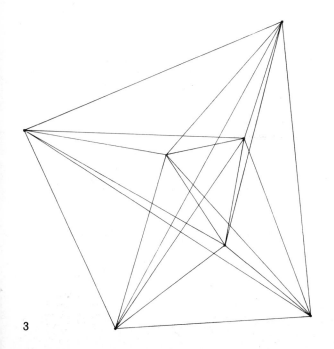

3

The range of linear designs, suitable for execution with pins and threads, is infinitesimal. The construction of a simple design, similar to figure 3, is self-evident; it consists merely in the joining together of each of the seven points to the other six.

But what of the more intricate design shown in figure 2. Although, at first sight, it might appear impossibly complex, it is, in principle, only an extension of the simple design of figure 3. Instead of seven points, this one has a hundred. Instead of the points being haphazardly arranged, they form the outline of a partially-constructed polygon; and instead of each point being joined to every other, only a proportion of possible linkages have been made In this first section, the development of linear design is traced from the simple example shown in figure 3 to the more complex one of figure 2, and some of the basic constructions are considered in an effort to understand the distinctive features which these constructions obtain.

Simple designs using an haphazard arrangement
of points.

4   Using 9 points

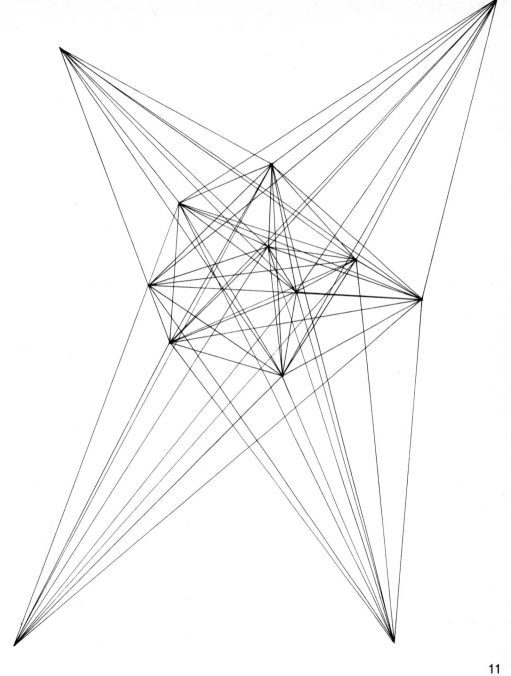

5 Using 13 points

The range and complexity of designs can be
extended by ordering some or all of the
haphazard points into regular lines, and linking
them with other haphazard points.
Figures 9 and 10 show the use of linked regular
lines of points only.

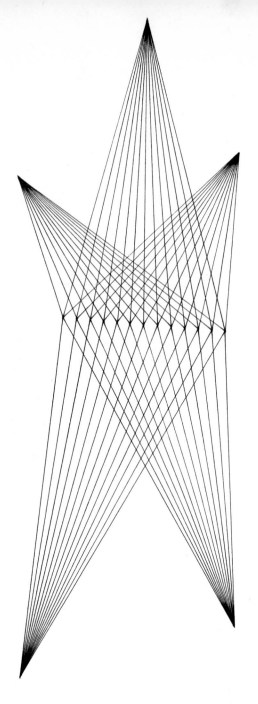

6

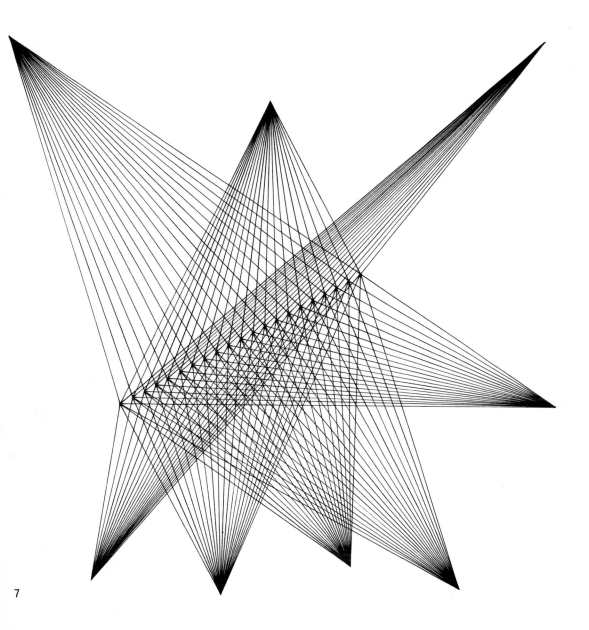

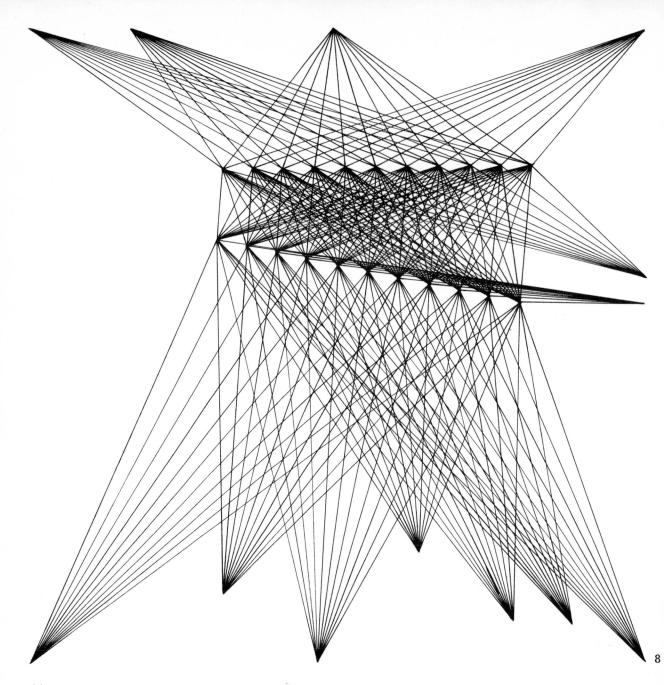

14

8

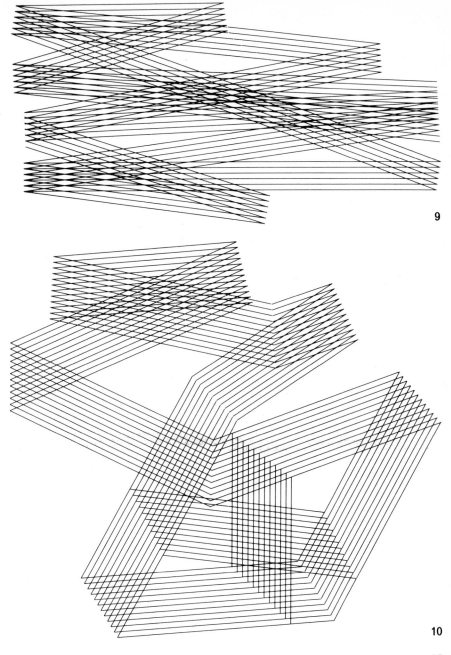

9

10

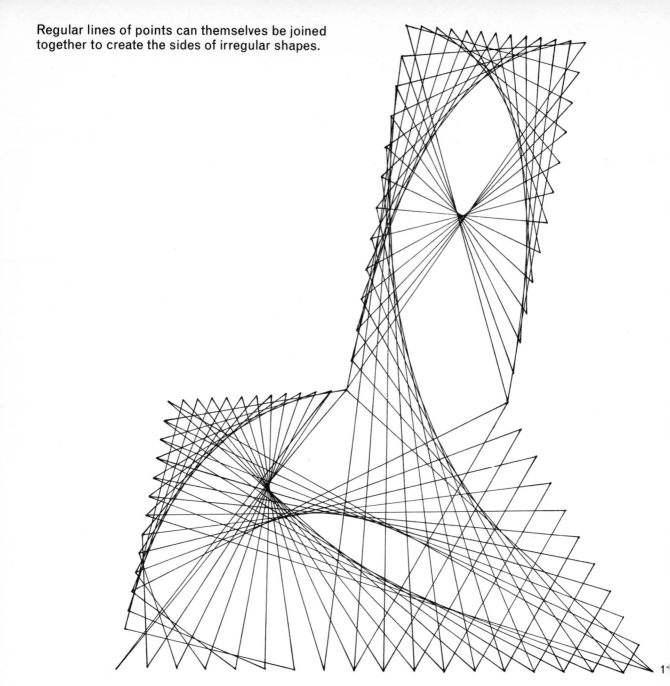

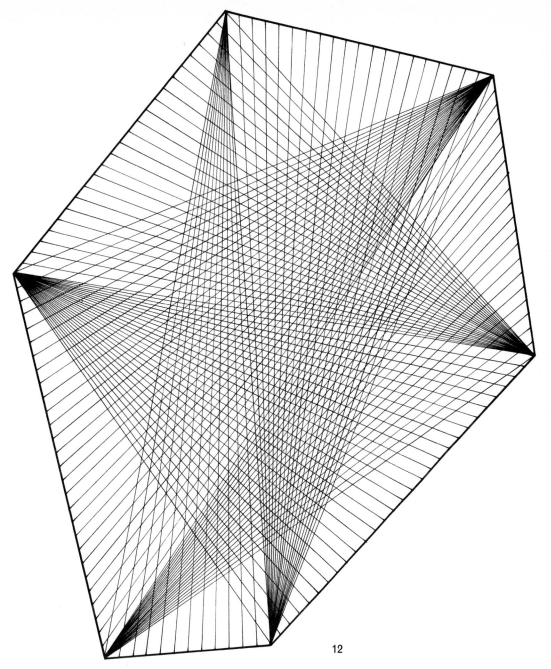

12

Regular shapes

Regular lines of points can be used to construct
regular shapes; squares, triangles, rectangles,
circles, spirals, polygons, etc; and these regular
shapes can be further subdivided to increase the
complexity of the design.

Figures 13 to 22 show some of the variety of
designs which can be achieved by joining together
points on a square or rectangle.

Figures 23 to 27 show the use of subdivided
squares; and figures 28 and 29, the use of
triangles.

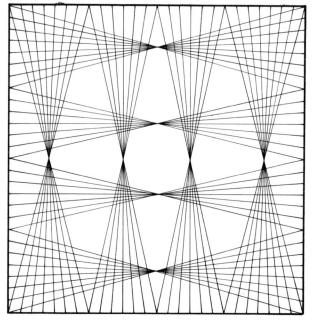

13

1

15

16

17

18

19

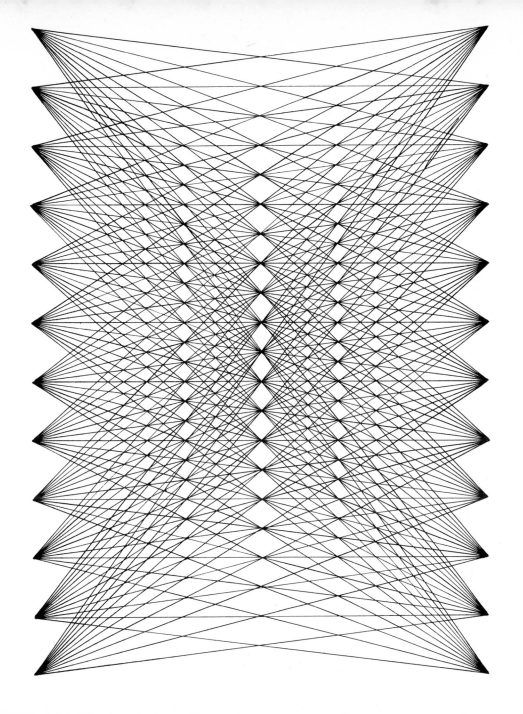

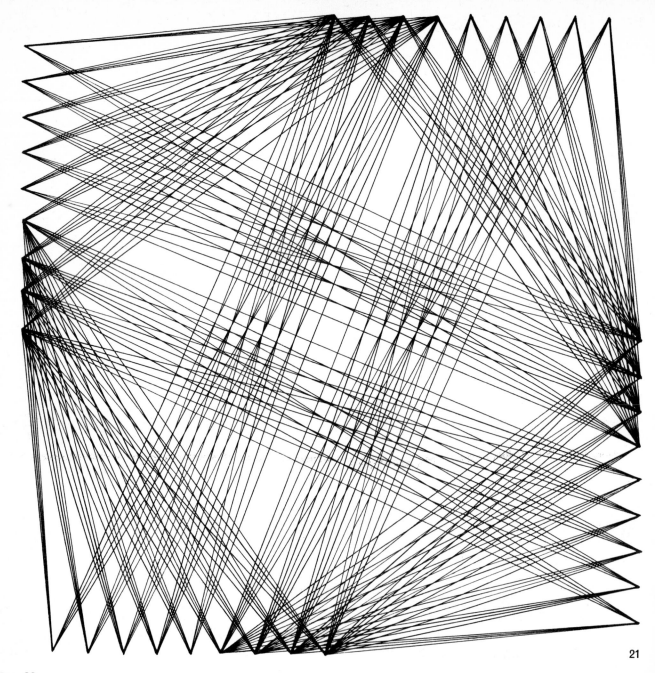

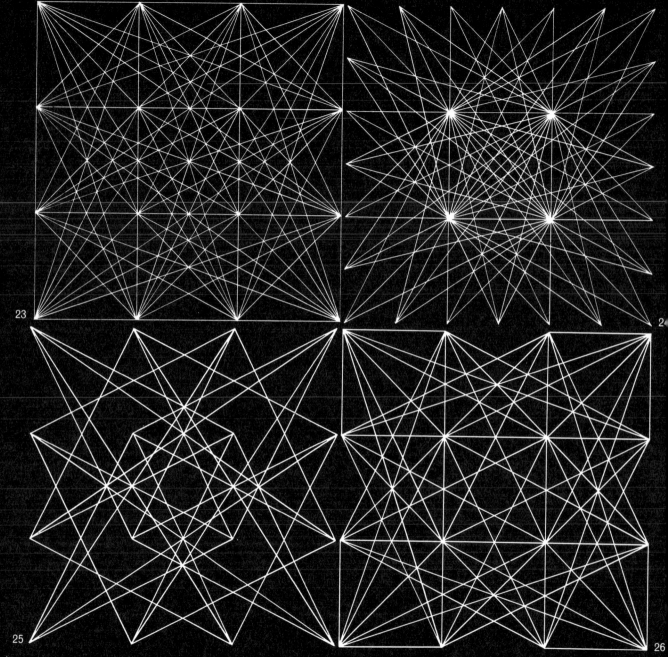

23

24

25

26

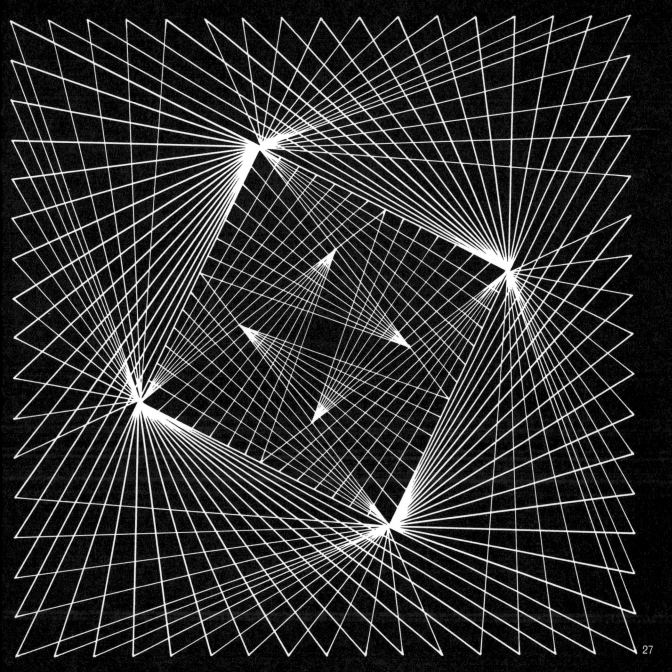

2

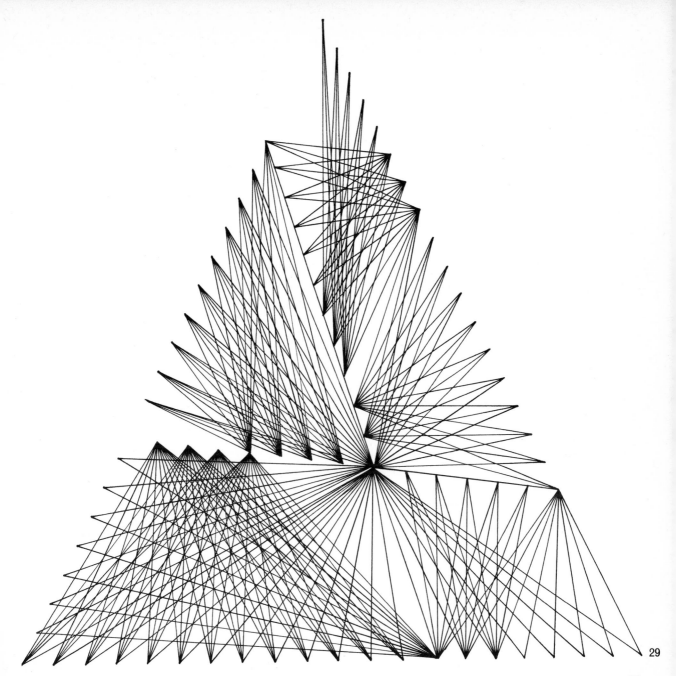

Circles

Figures 30 and 31 show the effects achieved by joining together pairs of points around the circumference of a circle. If, for example, the points of the circle opposite were numbered 1 to 57, then, by joining together numbers 1–23, 2–24, 3–25, and so on, around the circumference, the small circle would be formed. By joining together numbers 1–19, 2–20, 3–21 etc, the large inner circle is formed. Figures 32 to 35 show various designs based on a circle.

30

31

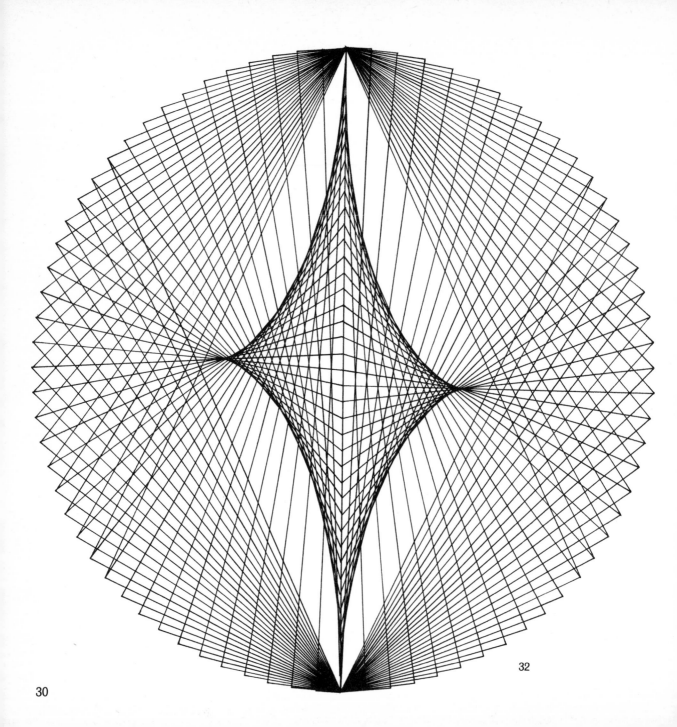

32

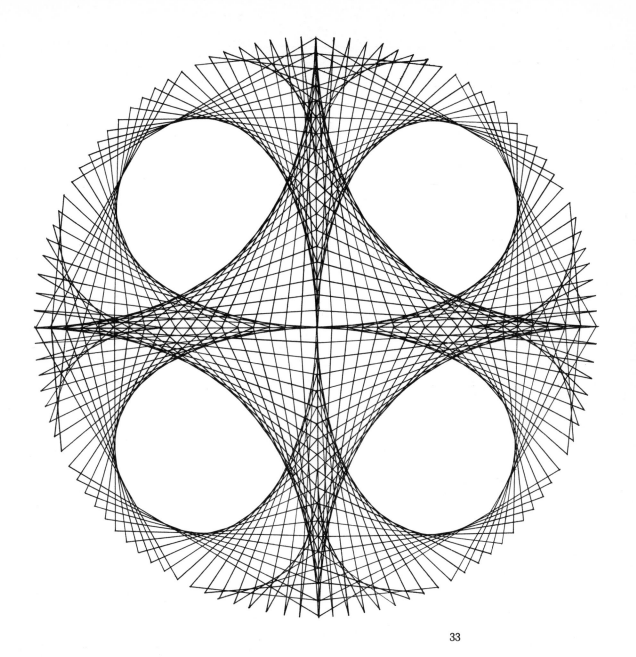

33

34

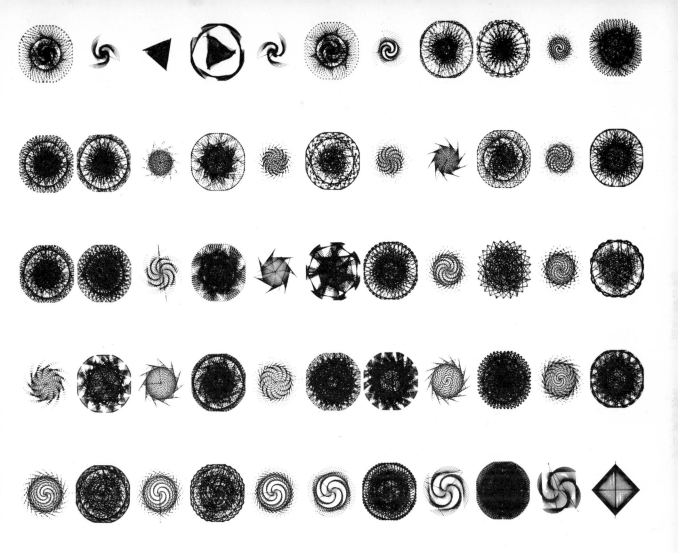

35   Sequences from the film *Per-mu-ta-tions* by John Whitney

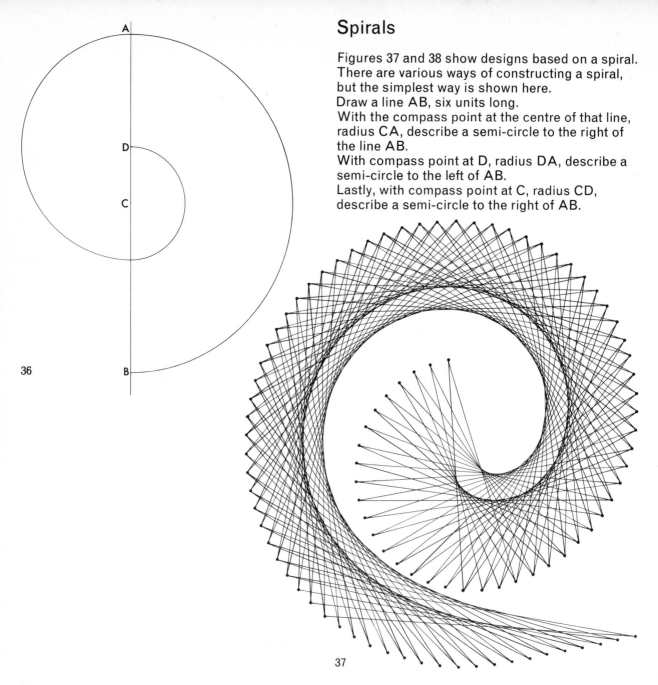

Spirals

Figures 37 and 38 show designs based on a spiral.
There are various ways of constructing a spiral,
but the simplest way is shown here.
Draw a line AB, six units long.
With the compass point at the centre of that line,
radius CA, describe a semi-circle to the right of
the line AB.
With compass point at D, radius DA, describe a
semi-circle to the left of AB.
Lastly, with compass point at C, radius CD,
describe a semi-circle to the right of AB.

36

B

37

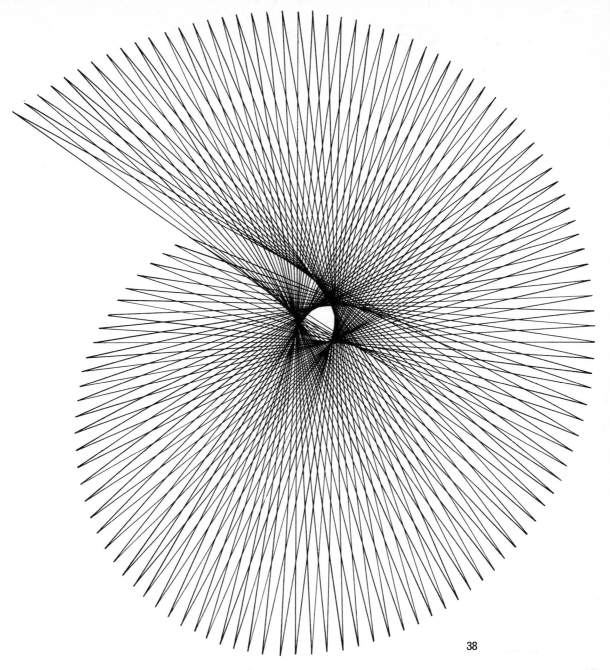

38

Polygons

To construct a regular six-sided polygon

Draw any circle, radius AC. Using the same compass radius, place the compass at any point on the circumference (for example, at C), and describe two arcs to intersect the circumference at B and E. Repeat again with the compass point at E, F, G and D. Join the points on the circumference together.

To construct a regular polygon with any number of sides

Draw a circle diameter AB. Divide the line AB into the same number of equal parts as the polygon has sides (for example, 7). With compass point at A and B, radius slightly larger than AB, describe arcs to intersect at C. Draw a line from C to pass through division 2, intersecting the circumference at D. The line AD is one seventh of the circumference. With a compass, radius AD, step off arcs around the circumference, and join the intersections together.

Figures 41 to 46 show examples of polygon-based designs.

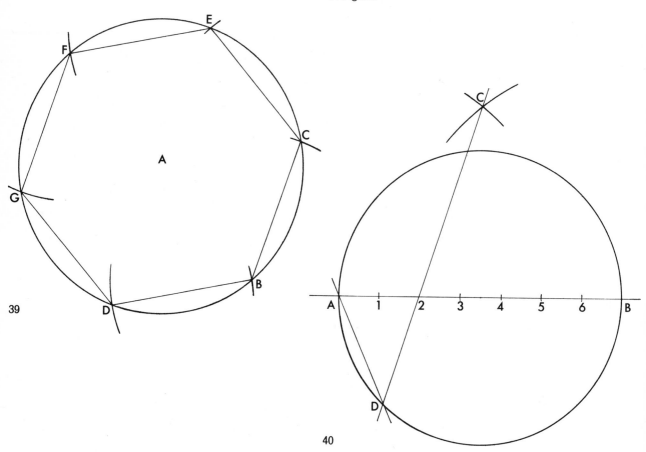

39

40

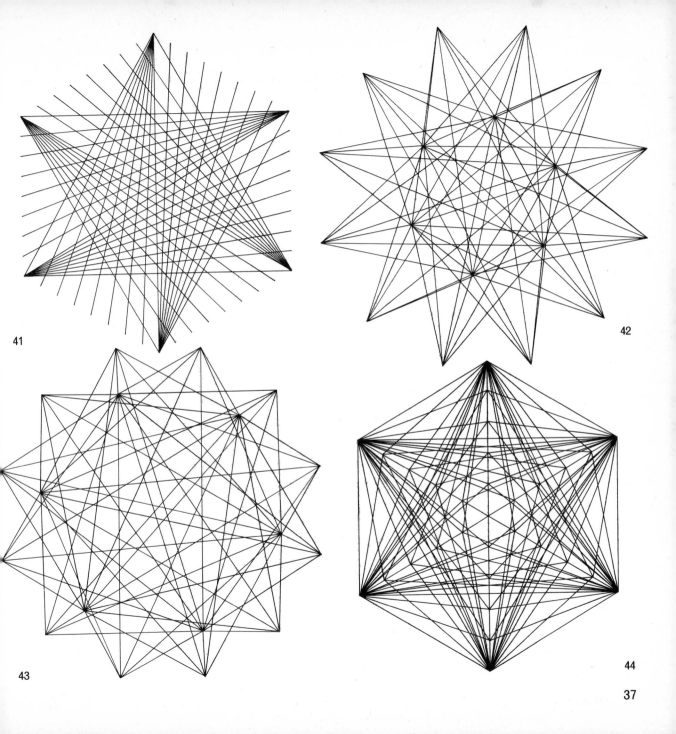

41

42

43

44

Moiré patterns

This rather complex and confusing visual effect can best be seen when two sets of parallel or regularly diverging lines are superimposed, nearly, but not quite, fully aligned. *Moiré* is a French word meaning 'watered', and was first used to describe the effect achieved in certain kinds of fabric, particularly silks and rayons – hence the term 'watered-silk'.

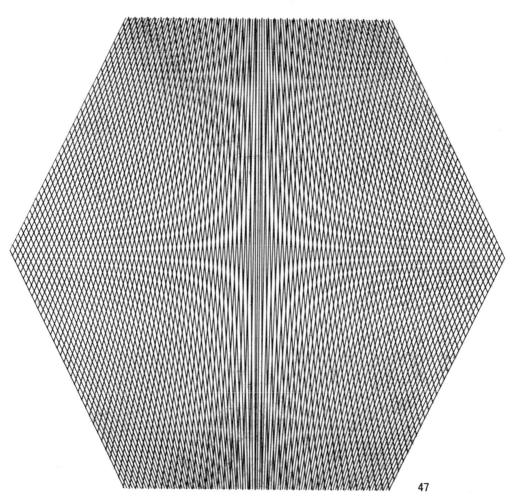

47

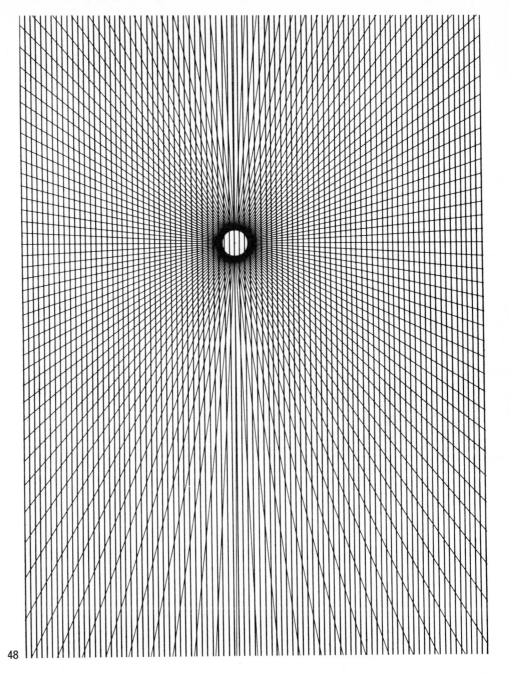

48

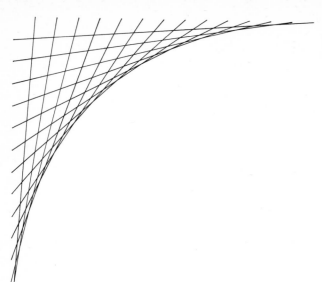

49

Curve stitching

One of the most interesting aspects of linear design concerns the creation of curved shapes from patterns of straight lines. The basic curve (figure 49) consists in the joining together of two lines of equidistant points set at right angles. This basic curve can be altered by changing the angle at which the two lines intersect (ie, by making the angle smaller, as in figure 50; or larger, as in figure 51); or by separating the two lines completely, as in figure 52. By drawing the curves in the angles of an enclosed shape of three or more lines, complete envelopes can be produced, as in figure 53.

Figures 54 to 62 show just some of the many possible curves which can be produced, and the ways in which they can be used together.

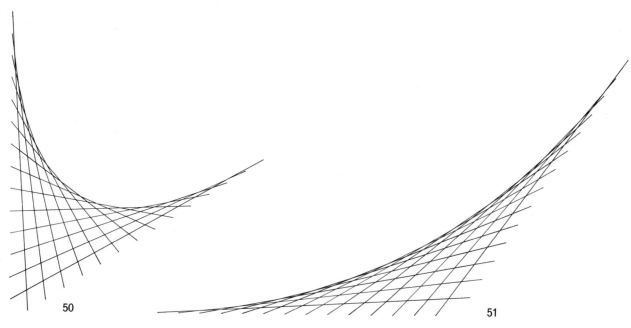

50

51

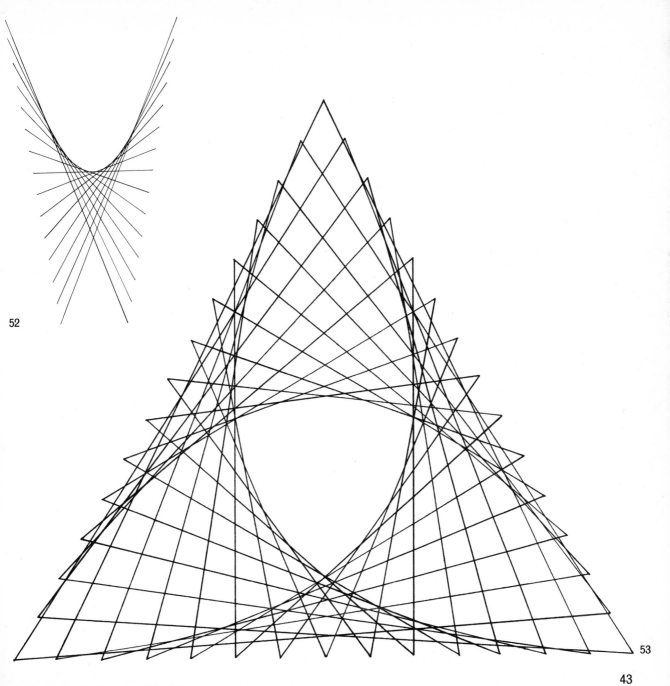

52

53

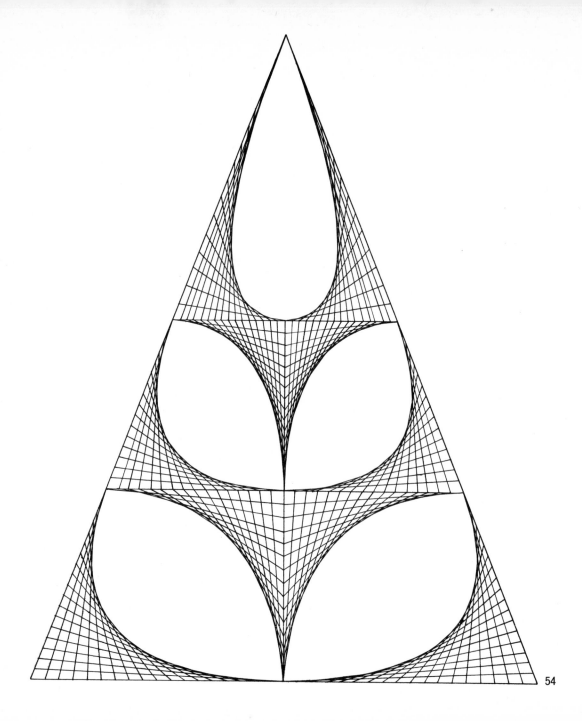

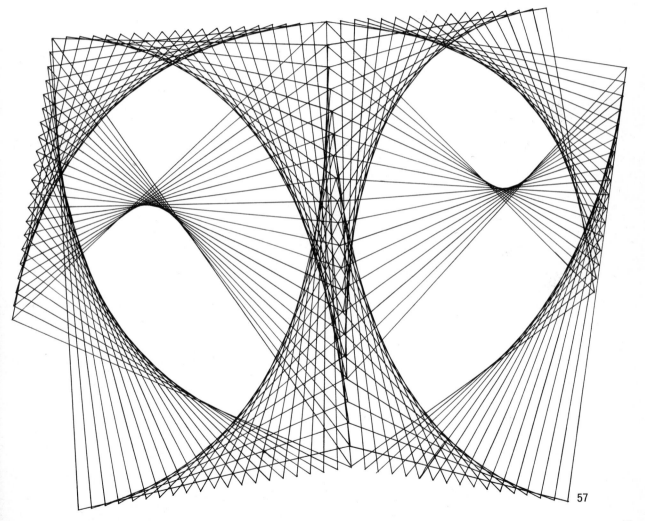

57

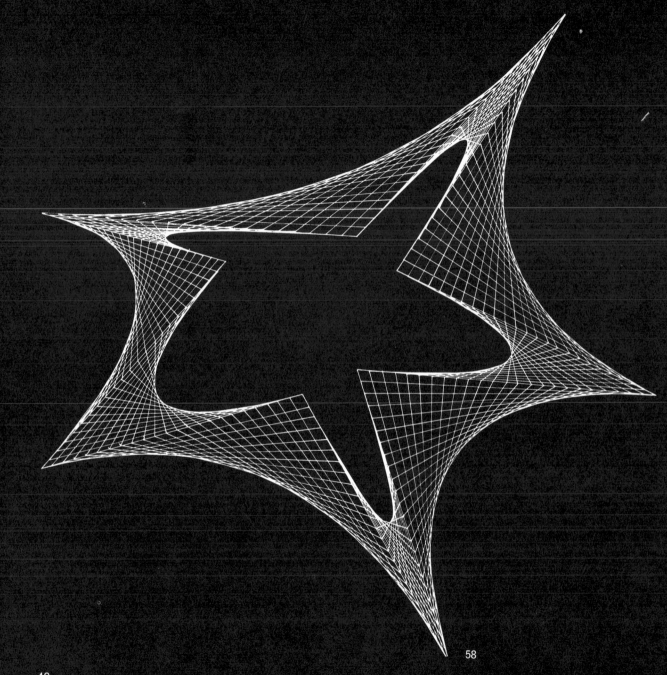

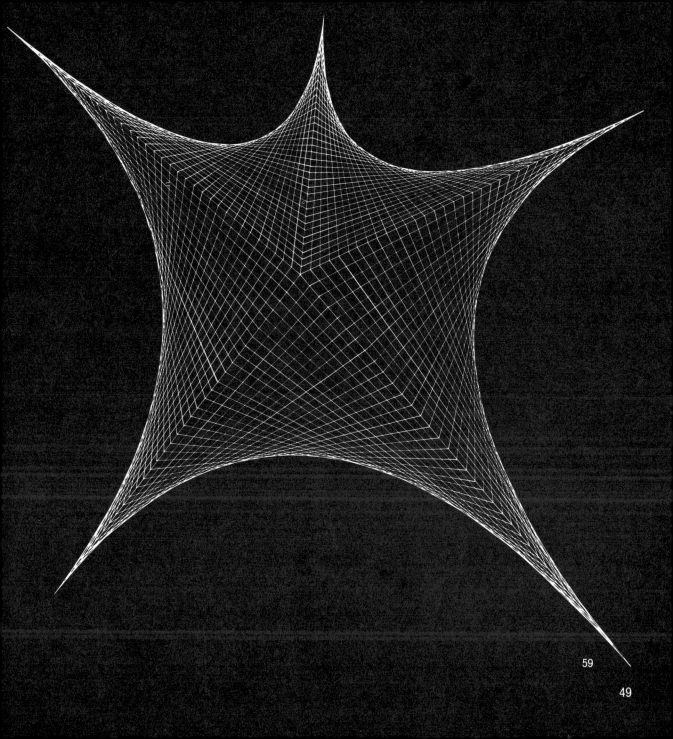

59

49

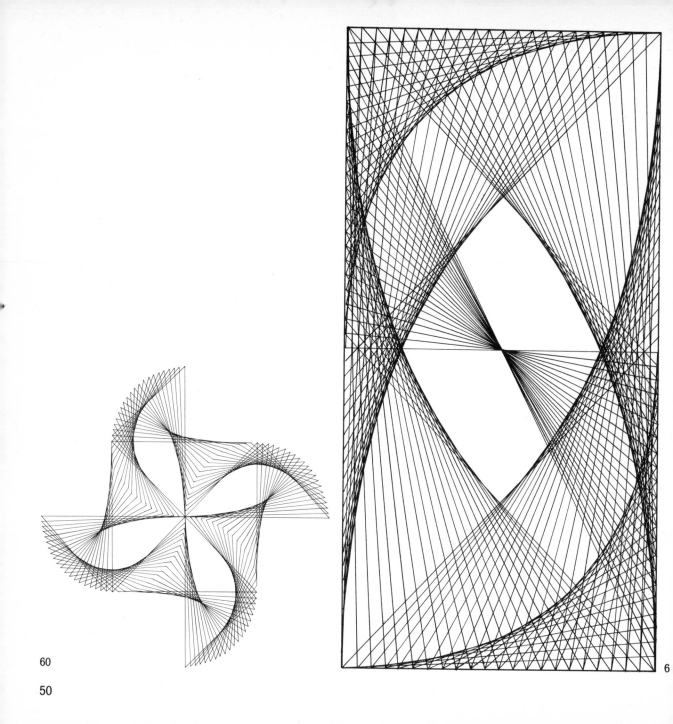

60

50

6

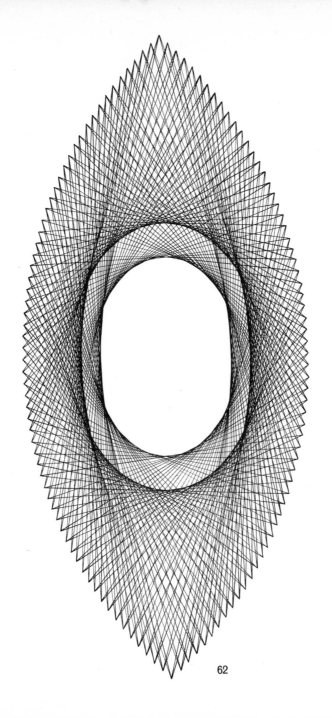

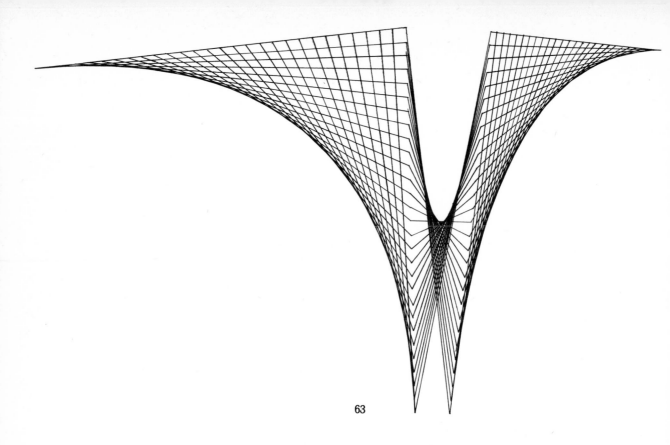

63

Representational design

It will be noticed how, by chance, certain
arrangements of lines and curves take on the
appearance of recognisable objects such as stars,
flowers and animals. For some the design above
is purely abstract; for others it is a bird in flight
– a seagull perhaps. But whatever image it
conjures up, the notion of representational design
itself provides a whole new range of possibilities.
Either, we can begin with a simple line drawing
(figure 64), and proceed to use the shape as a
design matrix (figure 65), or we can adapt and
rearrange the multiplicity of abstract forms to our
own representational ends, as in figures 66 to 71.

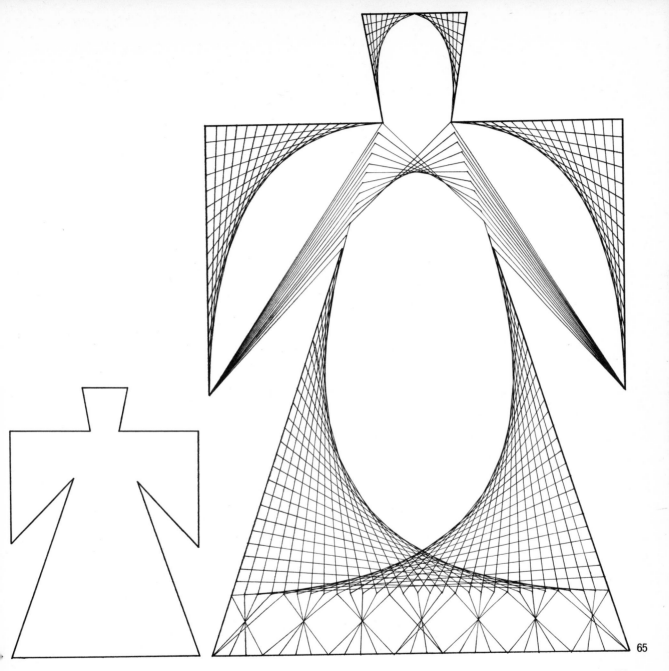

65

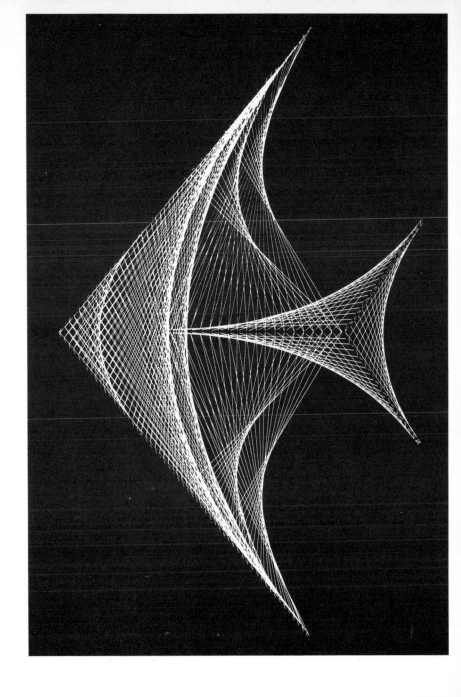

66   Angel Fish

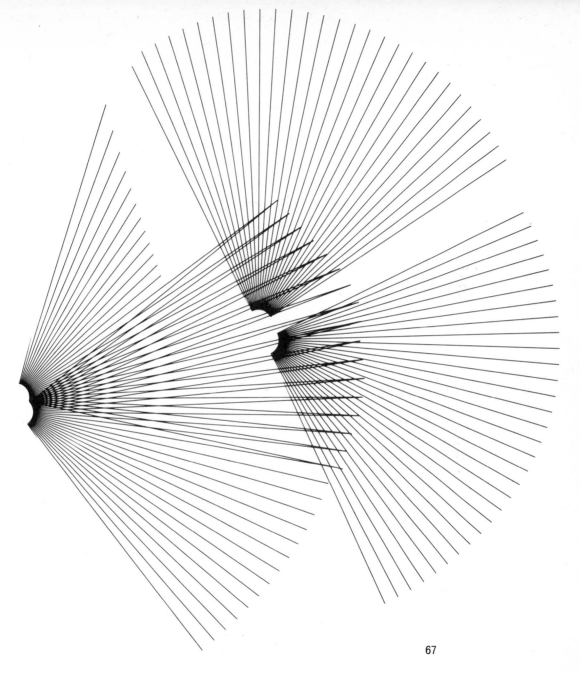

67

68

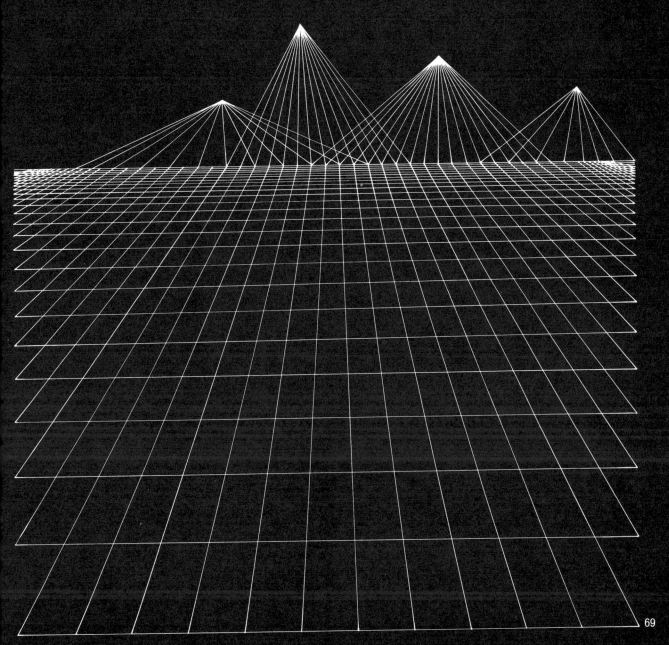

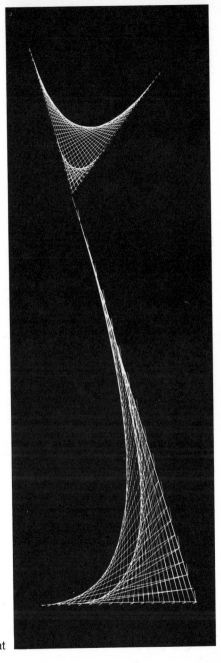

71 Siamese Cat

Linear design with threads and wire

So far the formal aspects of linear design have been considered. Now we turn to the practice of translating a line drawing into pins and thread; into the kind of decorative panel illustrated above.

Whatever the materials to be used – pins and thread, nails and wire – the technique is basically the same: difficulties which may arise result from the complexities of the effect to be created, or the particular materials involved.

To illustrate the technique, let us consider the method to be used in the making of the small pin and thread panel, figure 72.

Firstly, the materials involved
The base board
This must be a soft-bodied board (insulating board, for instance), in which fine steel pins can easily be embedded. Cut the board to the desired size, and smooth away any rough edges with fine sandpaper. If the board is to be painted, use 2 to 3 coats of any water-based or oil-based paint.
Pins and thread
A quantity of round-headed pins are needed, equal in number to the points required by the design, and a sufficient quantity of ordinary cotton, or sewing thread.
A working drawing
The drawing must merely show the positions of the points required, as in figure 73. It must be drawn to the same size as the board, on as thin a paper as possible.

Secondly, the method
1   Place the working drawing exactly over the panel, holding the drawing in place (if necessary) with adhesive tape or pins.

72

2   Half insert the pins through the points of the drawing into the panel.
3   Remove the drawing by tearing away.
4   Imagine that the points of the spiral are numbered from 1 to 97 (from the outer to the inner edge). Begin by knotting the cotton thread at point 1. Keeping the thread as taut as possible, take it around pin number 22, and back to pin number 2, then from 2–23, 23–3, 3–24, and so on, in sequence, using a continuous line of thread, finally fastening the end of the thread at pin number 97.
If the thread breaks, tie it off at the nearest convenient pin, and begin again from the same pin with a new reel or length of thread.
The design should now resemble figure 74.
5   Repeat the process, this time threading from 1–19, 19–2, 2–20, 20–3, and so on around the spiral to pin number 97.
The design should look like figure 75.
Last of all, fully insert all the pins to *secure* the thread.

73

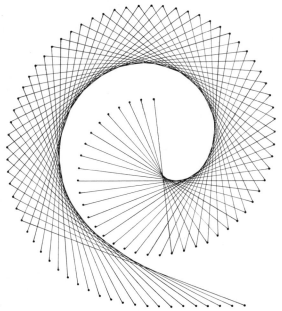

74

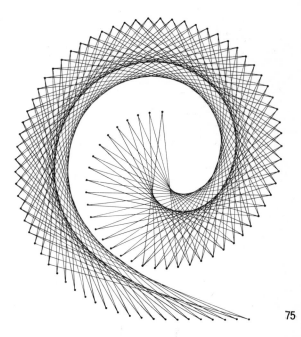

75

Working drawings

Not every thread panel requires the use of an exact full-size working drawing of the kind suggested above. There, its purpose was a strictly utilitarian one, making it possible to mark off the points where pins were required, without the necessity of making unsightly preliminary drawings on the surface of the panel itself.

But working drawings, whether drawn to scale or not, have a role to play in the design process as a whole. Clearly, it is cheaper and quicker to work out the design of a panel using pencil and paper than with copper nails and phosphor-bronze wire. Moreover, small pencilled designs can more easily be kept together (in a sketchbook or file system) to provide a ready source of ideas for later work. But perhaps most important of all, the habit of making working drawings develops a growing awareness of the possibilities inherent in linear design. For not every arrangement of lines or permutation of curves produces a satisfying result, and the experience gained from the working-out of designs in pencil and paper will directly affect the quality of work to be achieved with threads and wire.

Panel materials and preparation

A very wide range of materials suitable for creative work with wire and thread is available. Basically these materials can be divided into two groups; those suitable for use with pins, and those suitable for use with nails.

Of the materials suitable for work with pins (that is, materials soft enough for pins to be inserted by hand, or with a small hammer), one large group may be singled out – fibre building boards.

Fibre building boards themselves can be divided into two main groups;
1   non-compressed, lightweight insulating boards, softboards, and tiles

2 medium boards.

(Both groups are manufactured by a number of companies, each with their own individual trade names.)

Group 1

These are soft, fibrous, lightweight boards, ideally suited to receive pins, and soft enough to be used by young children. They are available in a variety of surface textures (from smooth to dimpled, although one or both sides may have a fabric-like texture); a variety of colours (all shades from off-white to light and dark brown); and a variety of surface treatments (painted, or faced with paper, aluminium, plastic, textile, etc). All these boards can be cut very easily with a hand-saw, or a sharp cutting knife, but care must be taken to smooth all roughened edges with fine sandpaper or wire wool.

Group 2

Medium boards (midway in hardness between hardboard and softboard) are available in a variety of surface textures (one side usually smooth, the other fabric-like); a variety of colours (from mid-grey to dark brown); and a variety of surface treatments (ivory faced, lacquered, painted, etc). Medium boards are easily cut with a hand saw, and require minimal smoothing-off with sandpaper.

Other materials suitable for use with pins, although considerably more expensive, include polystyrenes in various densities, and cork, now available in tiles.

Materials suitable for work with nails (in addition to the medium and hardboards) include woods of all kinds, woodwool slabs, plywoods, blockboards, laminates and chipboards.

Surface treatments

All of the materials mentioned above (whether for use with pins or nails) can be used in their natural state; indeed, in the case of most natural woods and cork, surface quality, colour and texture can play an important part in the design as a whole.

Elsewhere, the board surface may be painted or treated in some other way to complement the linear design of threads or wire.

(a) *Painting* Water-based paints (poster paint, tempera colour, polymers, acrylics, household emulsions, etc) are suitable for all the materials above, although the smooth-faced hardboards may require a preliminary coating of hardboard primer. In addition, experiment can be made with paints of other kinds (oil and spirit based paints, enamels, lacquers, etc) although these are usually more expensive.

(b) *Covering* Board surfaces can be wholly or partly covered with a variety of materials: papers of all kinds, fabric, plastic, tin foil, thin metal sheet (to be used with nails only), card, netting, etc.

76 *opposite* Polyester thread on felt covered chipboard
77 *below* Small pin and thread panel on an insulation board base
78 *overleaf* *Light Years of a Constellation* 1973 Jennifer Gray
79 *overleaf right* *Silver Cusp* 1969 Jennifer Gray

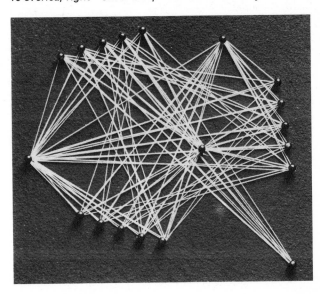

80

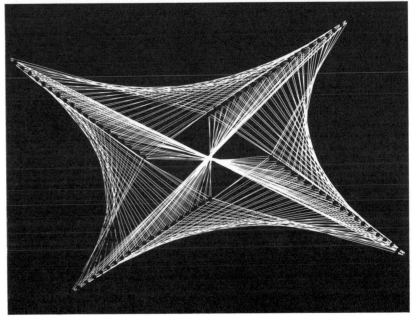

81

82 Nails may be divided into types in respect of size, shape of head, point, shank, metal type, coating and finish. The most common and useful types are:

1 round, plain head
2 round, lost head
3 box
4 oval, brad head
5 oval, lost head
6 lath
7 panel pins
8 clout or slate

Pins and nails

Two main types of pin are available:
(a)   the common small-headed pin, and
(b)   the round-headed pin.
Type (a) is available in a variety of sizes (up to 50 mm – 2 in.), and metals (steel, stainless steel, and brass).
Type (b) (predominantly steel) have a comparatively large, round, plastic head in a variety of colours.

Nail metals
Nails are made from various metals, steel being the most common, but interesting effects can be achieved using non-rusting nails of brass, copper, stainless steel, and aluminium.

Metal coatings and finishes
Different coatings and finishes may be applied to steel nails to reduce corrosion and improve appearance. The most common coatings and finishings are: galvanised, copper/tin/brass/cadmium/nickel/chromium plated, blued, japanned, and painted.

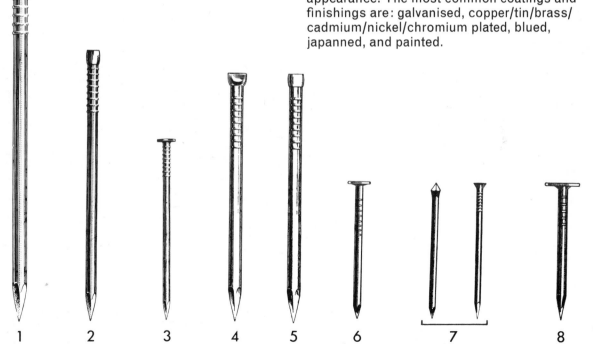

1   2   3   4   5   6   7   8

Wire and thread

Conventional linear designs can be worked-out in a range of threads and wires, bearing in mind that the thread should be strong enough to support tension.

Ordinary cotton sewing thread and thin copper or steel wire will doubtless provide the basis for

83 Goldfingering thread on a background of black felt

most designs, but the range of other materials
must not be overlooked:
wool, yarn, weaving threads, tapestry threads,
nylon, polyester, lurex threads in metallic colours
fine cords and string, and wires in various
metals: the list is endless. (Other, less
conventional materials are referred to on page 77.)

84   *Multiple Shell* 1969 Jennifer Gray

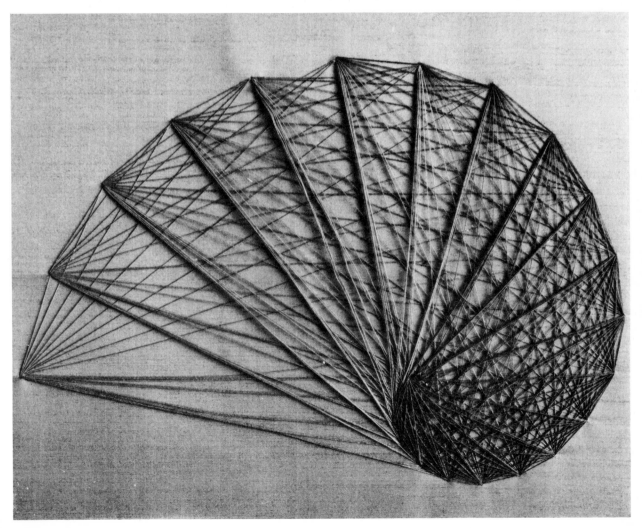

85

87 *opposite*   *String Composition* 1964 Sue Fuller
The Tate Gallery, London

8

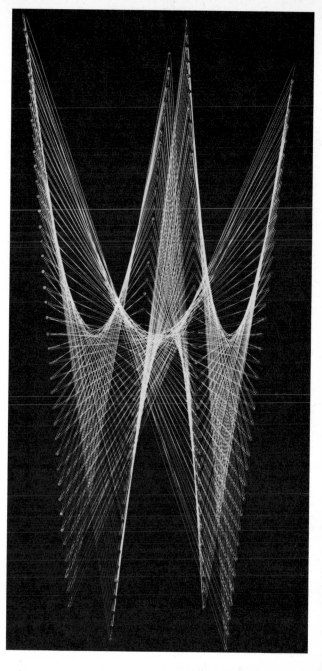

88

Development of linear design

Apart from two-dimensional compositions using threads and wire, there are a variety of ways in which this basic aspect might further be developed and explored.

Working drawings in pen or pencil can be seen as sufficient in themselves, to be exploited in other materials – a scratched line drawing on slate, or an impressed line design in clay. The use of myriad lines of thread suggests affinities with weaving, tapestry, linear sculpture, optical art, and the like, and suggest possibilities with other materials – cane, metal rod, paper string, etc. Even the use of nails and pins themselves offers scope for further experiment with textural design and sculpture in two and three dimensions.

Opposite is mapped out just some of these possibilities. They illustrate the very wide range of creative work which these materials and techniques present.

Other linear materials and material treatments

Interesting and varied effects can be achieved through experiment with materials other than wire or thread, some of which necessitate large scale treatments.
Various ropes and strings: sisal, manilla, jute, etc
Raffia, seagrass, cane
Paper string and paper strip

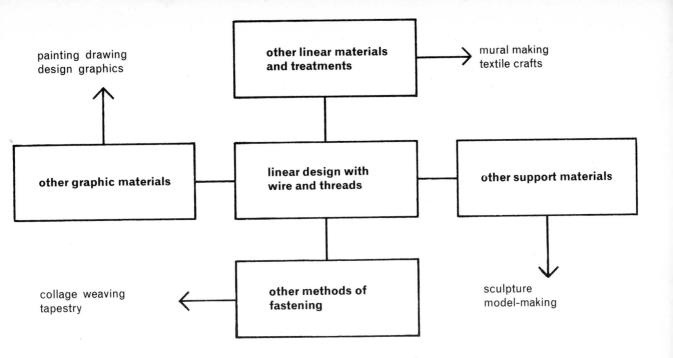

Nylon thread, ribbons, tapes, magnetic recording tape
Elastic bands, pipe cleaners, drinking straws, etc
Many of these materials can be further exploited by knotting, twisting, plaiting etc.

Other graphic media

Most working drawings will be made on paper in pencil, felt tip or ball point pen, but a whole new range of effects presents itself when we consider the use of different supports and different drawing media. Furthermore, we can see experiments in this area not merely as 'working drawings' but as linear creations in their own right.
Other supports: graph paper, slate, wood, fabric, etc
Other media: chalk, crayon, charcoal, coloured ink, paint, etc

Other support materials

As well as the variety of boards and supports which are suitable for use with pins and nails, there are other methods of fastening which make possible the use of a much wider range of support materials.
Thick paper, card, strawboard, etc
Open-mesh fabrics and metals; jute, hessian, sackcloth, netting, old pieces of knitted fabric, metal gauze, wire netting, expanding metal meshes, etc
Perforated hardboards and zinc sheet
Wooden frames, boxes, etc
The range can be extended still further by using three-dimensional, as opposed to two-dimensional supports. Three-dimensional frames of various kinds can be constructed in wood, wire, metal, cane, plastic, cardboard, etc.

90–91 Linear designs used as a matrix for filling in with colour Spyros Horemis

77

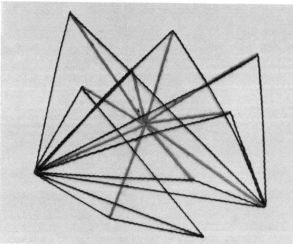

92 *above* Cotton threaded design on stiff card
93 *left* Wood threaded design on paper

Other methods of fastening

Depending on the kind of support material being used, other fastening techniques are possible.
A notched or unnotched edge of card or wood
A pierced material; for example, needle holes in a piece of card
Pre-perforated materials, such as hardboard or zinc
Other 'nail-like' fasteners, such as wooden pegs in perforated hardboard, screws, staples, drawing pins, etc
Open-mesh materials and fabrics, such as wire netting or open weave canvas

94 *above* A large decorative panel using a variety of threads and strings, interwoven with knotted cord, buttons and beads.

95 *left* Card-based design used as a basis for figurative interweaving with thick wools, ribbons and tapes.

Instead of using pins and nails on stiff board, linear designs can be threaded through pierced holes into paper, card, or thin plastic.

Linear designs can be created by wrapping cotton thread, string, wool, etc, around a simple geometric shape of card or hardboard, and using the pattern of threads as a weaving frame to be interwoven with other materials.

79

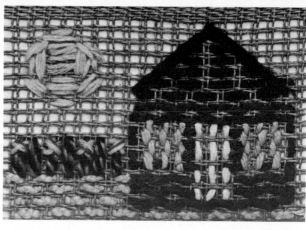

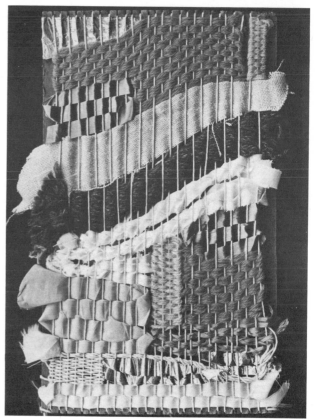

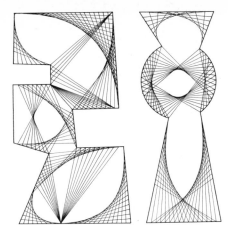

The technique illustrated in figures **94** and **95** can further be extended by using abstract or agurative shaped supports. Simple shapes like these serve as an admirable introduction to linear design for young children, quite apart from their obvious relationships with weaving and tapestry.

96 *opposite left*   *Macrogauze 29* **1969** Peter Collingwood
97 *opposite above*   Woven design on carpet canvas
98 *opposite below*   Woven design on a simple weaving frame
99 *left*   Abstract-shaped supports
100 *below*   Figurative-shaped support

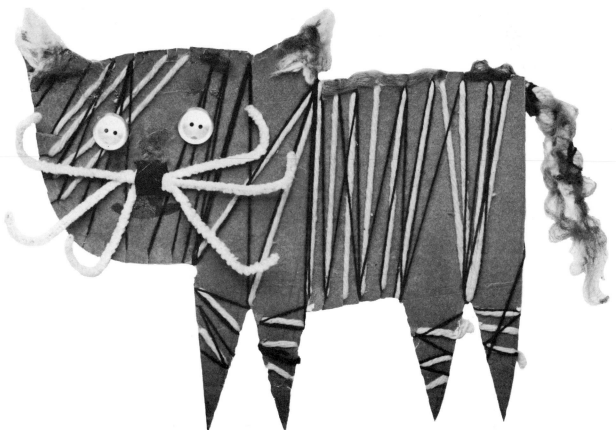

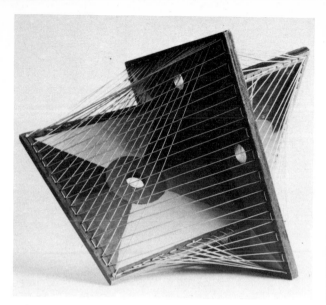

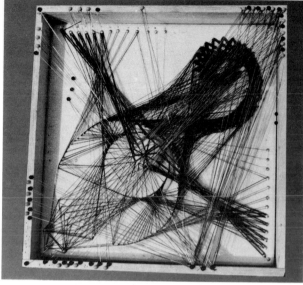

101 *above left*   Design by Edward Rogers
102 *above right*   Box construction
103 *left*   Three-dimensional weaving frame
104 *opposite*   *Linear Construction* 1942–3 Plastic with
plastic threads Naum Gabo The Tate Gallery, London

Linear design in three dimensions

A whole new area of possibilities is presented
when the concept of linear design is translated
into three-dimensional terms. Figures 102 and 103
show two of the simplest ways of developing this
idea, by using an open framework of cardboard or
wood (an old shoe box, cardboard boxes of all
sizes, or specially-constructed frames from
various materials), or an enclosing frame to serve
as an integral part of a two-dimensional panel.

Yet the idea can be extended indefinitely, as the
following illustrations show; from the welded
sculpture of Pevsner, to the linear complexities of
Richard Lippold's *Flight*.

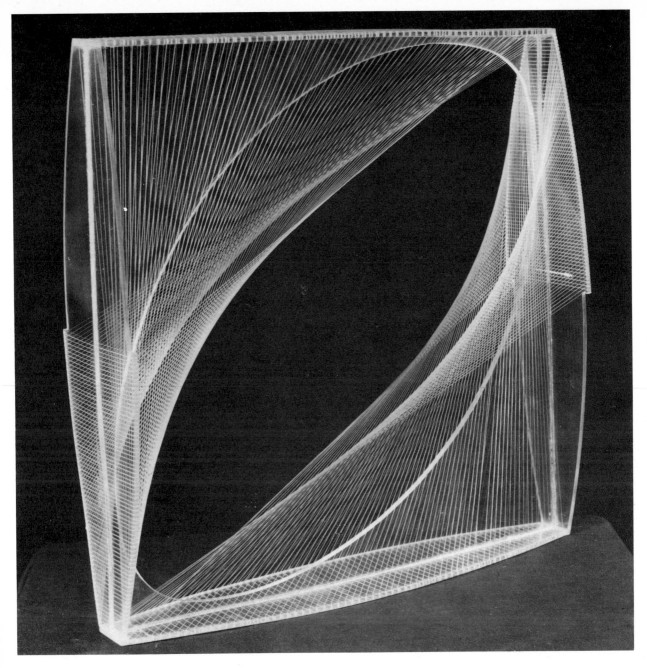

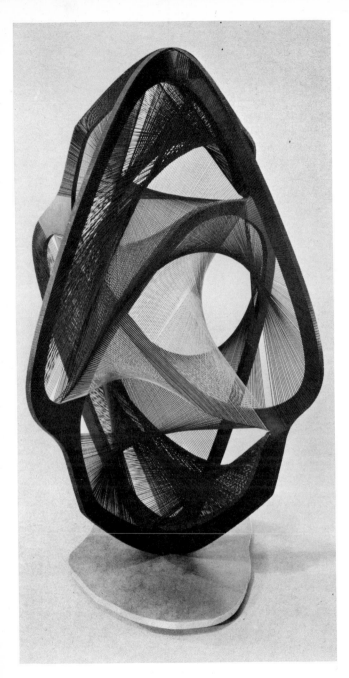

105 *opposite* Maquette of a Monument symbolising the Liberation of the Spirit 1952 Bronze Antoine Pevsner The Tate Gallery, London
106 *left* Linear Construction No 4 *in black and grey* 1953 aluminium and stainless steel The Art Institute of Chicago, gift of Mrs Suzette Morton Zurcher
107 *overleaf* Detail of *Flight* 1963 Richard Lippold Pan-Am Building, New York

Nail art

No one who has explored the techniques so far described can have overlooked the often exciting visual effects created by the pattern and shadows of pins or nails before the threads are added. Indeed, for many artists and craftsmen, the creation of such effects becomes an involvement in itself.

The range of work possible in this area is clearly far too wide to be treated in detail, but the examples of work shown here, from simple experiments in pattern and texture using pins of various kinds pressed into or fastened onto balsa wood or polystyrene tiles, and small three dimensional designs using pins, to the mature work of practising artists such as David Partridge and Dusan Dzamonja, should illustrate the wide range of developments which are possible.

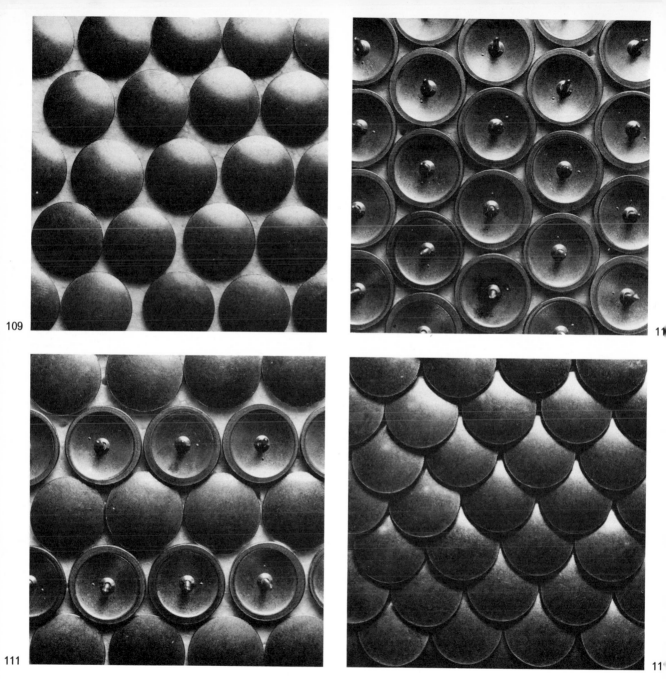

109

11

111

11

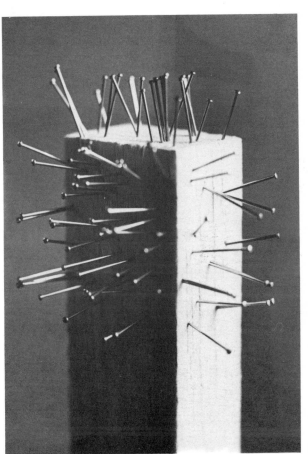

113

117 *Asteroids* David Partridge   Leicester Education Authority
118 *opposite left*   *Vertebrate Configuration* 1963 David Partridge   The Tate Gallery, London
119 *opposite right*   *Metal Sculpture 14* Steel, Brass and bronze rods Dusan Dzamonja

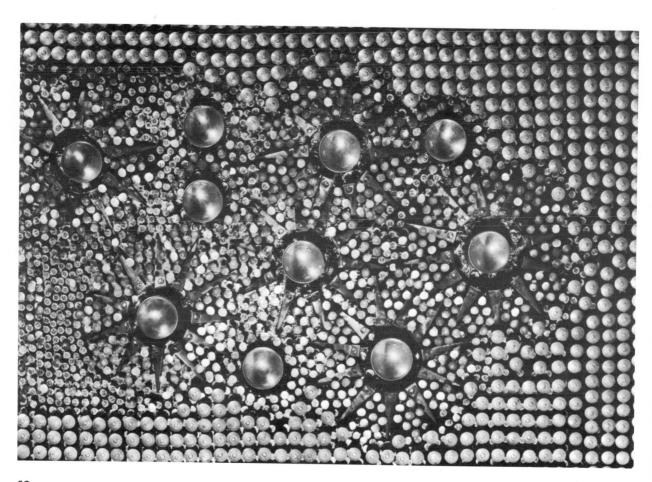

120 Textile printing block of the late eighteenth century. Prior to the adaptation of engraved copper plates for the use of textile printing in the nineteenth century, fine line and dotted effects were achieved with blocks such as this – the design being picked out with hundreds of small copper nails (less frequently, copper strips) embedded in wooden blocks.

Though clearly not intended as three-dimensional pin sculptures in their own right, they provide a very genuine inspiration to the creative artists of today

Suppliers

Threads etc

Artwork Needlework Industries Ltd
7 St Michael's Mansions   Ship Street
Oxford OX1 3DG
(Decorative threads of all kinds)

Louis Grossé Ltd
36 Manchester Street   London W1M 5PE
(Gold, silver, and metal threads)

Nottingham Handcraft Company
(School Suppliers)
Melton Road   West Bridgford
Nottingham NG2 6HD

Royal School of Needlework
25 Princess Gate   London SW7 1QE

J Hyslop Bathgate and Co
Galashiels   Scotland
(Wools)

Pins, nails, wire

A very wide range of materials will be available
from local stockists; haberdashers, hardware
stores, builders merchants, educational suppliers,
etc.

Board supports

Standard insulating and medium boards,
plywoods and composition boards are generally
available from builders merchants and hardware
stores; specialist suppliers include:

Cape Universal Building Products Ltd
Exchange Road   Watford WD1 7EQ

Nevill Long Group
North Hyde Wharf   Hayes Road
Southall   Middlesex

Sundeala Board Co Ltd
3 Aldwych   London WC2B 4BZ

Mace and Nairn
89 Crane Street   Salisbury
Wiltshire

Kit suppliers

The following companies supply complete 'linear design' kits containing all the basic materials which are required to construct a two-dimensional decorative panel

Thread sculpture
Westby Products
School Lane   East Keswick
Leeds LS17 9EH
(figures 1, 66, 71, 76, 85, 86, 88 manufactured by Bycra Ltd, Sandbeck Way, Wetherby: available from Westby Products)

Structural harmonographs
Wirecraft Enterprises
84 High Street   Colliers Wood
London SW19
(see figures 70, 80, 81)

Pin art
H G Twilley Limited,
Roman Mill
Stamford
Lincolnshire
from whom brochures may be obtained
(see figures 83, 89)

Thomas Salter Ltd
Woodside Road   Glenrothes
Fife KY7 4AG
supply three-dimensional linear design kits, based on a plastic frame

These kits are also obtainable from
The Needlewoman Shop
146 Regent Street   London W1
and many department stores and craft shops throughout the country